A Perspectives Flip Book

PUNISHING BULLIES:

Zero Tolerance vs.

Working Together

by Lisa Owings

Content Consultant
Amanda B. Nickerson, PhD
Associate Professor and Director
Alberti Center for Bullying Abuse Prevention
University at Buffalo, State University of New York

COMPASS POINT BOOKS
a capstone imprint

Compass Point Books are published by Capstone,
1710 Roe Crest Drive
North Mankato, Minnesota 56003
www.capstonepub.com

Editorial Credits
Melissa York, editor; Becky Daum and Craig Hinton, designers; Maggie Villaume,
production specialist; Catherine Neitge and Ashlee Suker, consulting editor
and designer

Photo Credits
Zero Tolerance
AP Images: Ed Andrieski, 13, *Houston Chronicle*/Karen Warren, 23, Tony Dejak,
25; Red Line Editorial, 24; Shutterstock Images: Monkey Business Images, 17,
Robynrg, 21, Shae Cardenas, 6; Thinkstock: Fuse, cover, Hermera, 5, iStock, 18,
Lite Productions, 11

Working Together
Alamy: Zuma Press, Inc., 27; AP Images: *Canadian Press*/Andrew Vaughan, 25,
Republic/Joe Harpring, 19; iStockphoto: ClarkandCompany, 12, Lokibaho, 17;
Shutterstock Images, Malyugin, cover, Monkey Business Images, 9, Olaf Speier, 6,
oliveromg, 5; Thinkstock: Fuse, 11, iStock, 23

Library of Congress Cataloging-in-Publication Data
Cataloging-in-publication information is on file with the Library of Congress.
ISBN 978-0-7565-4995-4 (library binding)
ISBN 978-0-7565-5048-6 (ebook PDF)
ISBN 978-0-7565-5044-8 (paperback)

Printed in the United States of America in Stevens Point, Wisconsin.
092014   008479WZS15

TABLE OF CONTENTS

Shared Resources

Chapter 1

BEING BULLIED

Every day millions of children around the world are bullied. For many, every bus ride to school, every break between classes, and every glance at a cell phone or computer screen fills them with terror. They sit on the bus or in the lunchroom trying to make themselves invisible, every moment expecting the next round of verbal or physical abuse.

The constant fear and anxiety takes an unfair toll on victims of bullying. Instead of focusing on learning at school, victims are preoccupied with basic safety. Often they try to avoid their bullies by pretending to be sick, skipping classes, or dropping out of school altogether. Even when victims are in their own homes, bullies can still reach them through texting and social media. The physical and emotional effects of bullying can haunt victims for the rest of their lives.

Victims' Stories

A boy from Iowa who loved learning was nervous about going to school because he had trouble making friends. He was skinny and had Asperger's syndrome, and people with that condition often have trouble interacting with others. Waiting quietly at the bus stop earned him threats from other boys. But that was nothing compared

Bullying can cause fear and unhappiness.

with what happened when he boarded the bus. The kids sitting near him threatened him, called him names, punched him, and stole things from him. They sat on him, choked him, and stabbed him with pencils, all because he looked and acted different. The bullying happened almost daily and went on for years.

One day the boy's class was learning about friendship. His teacher asked her students to raise their hands if they had at least two friends. The boy looked around as nearly everyone else stretched their hands into the air. The closest thing *he* had to friends were his bullies. "Most kids don't want to be around me," he said later. "I feel like I belong somewhere else."

A middle school boy living in New York State felt the same way. He was bullied because other kids thought he was gay. He had a high-pitched voice, and he made feminine gestures when he walked or talked. His classmates called him names and taped mean notes to his locker for all to see. Groups of boys teased him in the locker room. Later they stole his clothes from his locker and threw them in the trash. Kids also smashed his iPod and cell phone and wrote "I hope you die" on his shoes. The bullying continued through texts and phone calls when he went home. At least one of the boy's teachers also told him to stop acting so different from other boys.

The boy stayed true to himself, dying his hair pink or purple and sometimes wearing eyeliner or nail polish.

It can be difficult for people who are bullied to be themselves.

When he officially came out as gay, he hoped the bullies would leave him alone. Instead, they got more violent. They pushed him down the stairs, causing him to sprain his ankle. They tried to trip him in the hall while he was still on crutches. One boy threatened him with a pocketknife. When the bullied boy tried to fight back, he was punished. When his parents begged the school to intervene, nothing happened. The principal said that without adult witnesses or camera footage, the bullying couldn't be proved. The boy became depressed and started skipping school. His family and his best friend were the only people who seemed to accept him for who he was.

A new freshman girl at a school in Massachusetts felt accepted at first. She was smart and funny, outgoing and pretty. Teachers praised her as a star student, and girls were quick to befriend her. She also got plenty of attention from boys. Her relationship with two senior boys—and their current and former girlfriends—grew complicated, then ugly. The girls began calling her filthy names on Facebook. Soon they were harassing her at school, publicly shaming her and threatening to beat her up. Classrooms, hallways, the gym, the cafeteria, the library—nowhere was safe. Some days she skipped classes and took shelter in the nurse's office. Her mother, friends, and teachers could see that the situation was getting out of hand, but none of them knew how to help.

On a particularly bad day, the new girl was insulted in front of her friends, and one of the boys she had been involved with laughed and made fun of her. As she was leaving school, this boy and a couple of girls taunted her until she was in tears. Minutes later a car rolled past. A girl opened the window to hurl hate-filled words and an empty soda can at her. When the new girl got home, she texted a friend: "I can't do it anymore." That afternoon, she took her own life.

These stories provide a small glimpse into the struggles many victims of bullying face every day. Children who bully tend to pick on kids they see as different. Since every child is unique, anyone can be singled out as a victim. Kids are bullied for all kinds of reasons—the clothes they wear, the friends they choose, their sexual orientation, their skin color, their intelligence, and many more.

Bullied kids are more likely to experience depression and anxiety, among other problems. In some cases, the problems last into adulthood. In the rarest and most extreme cases, bullying victims never get past the bullying and other hardships of adolescence. Instead of reaching out for help or finding healthy ways to cope, they make the tragic and permanent decision to end their lives. Suicide is *never* a solution. When it happens, it can be a wake-up call for communities. Such tragedies have inspired governments and schools around the world to crack down on bullying.

Steps Forward

The boy who was bullied on the bus moved with his family to a different community and a different school. His family hopes to work with the families of other bullying victims to help stop bullying in schools. The boy has more support and many more friends at his new school.

With the help of his parents and the legal system, the boy who was bullied for being gay brought about change in his make schools safer for children of all sexual orientations.

After the new girl's death, her bullies were charged with multiple crimes. The bullies were sentenced to community service, while the most serious charges were dropped. The case increased awareness of the dangers of bullying. It also helped motivate the state of Massachusetts to pass laws that would help stop bullying.

Chapter 2

BULLYING: A SERIOUS THREAT

There is no universal definition for bullying. However, most experts agree bullying involves intentionally hurtful actions that are repeated over time. People who bully have physical or emotional power over their victims. This power imbalance makes it hard for victims to stand up for themselves.

Bullying takes many forms. It can be calling the new girl names or threatening to beat up the skinny boy at the bus stop. It can be spreading rumors online about the girl with a learning disability or the boy who wears pink. It can be excluding less popular kids from games at recess. It can be hitting the brown-skinned boy in the bathroom or throwing food at the girl who sits by

Size is one example of a power imbalance
between bullies and their victims.

herself in the lunchroom. Bullying can be physically or
emotionally hurtful. Often, it is both.

Most bullying happens at school in places where
adults are not watching. School hallways, bathrooms,
playgrounds, and buses are hot spots. And sometimes
bullies strike outside of school. Cyberbullying takes place
online or through text messages. That means bullying can
happen almost anytime, anywhere.

Getting Serious about Bullying

Many people see bullying as relatively harmless. They feel
it is something painful but necessary for kids to go through
on their way to adulthood. After all, how else would kids
learn how to handle everyday conflict?

Parents and teachers often tell bullied kids to stop being so sensitive or learn to stand up for themselves. Some blame the victims for not blending in. For instance, a North Carolina boy was being bullied for carrying a My Little Pony backpack. Some of his classmates thought the backpack was girly. The school initially told the boy to leave his backpack at home instead of addressing the bullying. Reactions like these send the message that bullying is OK.

The "kids will be kids" attitude toward bullying was once even more common. It was not until the mid-20th century that things started changing. In the early 1970s, a professor of psychology published the first scientific research on bullying. Dan Olweus' efforts helped bring international attention to the issue. His studies suggested that bullying was a serious problem, not unavoidable child behavior.

In 1982 northern Europeans were shocked by the suicides of three young Norwegian boys ages 10 to 14. All appeared to have been victims of brutal bullying, and public reaction was to link the two. Norwegians knew they had to take swift action to prevent similar tragedies. So in 1983 the Norwegian Ministry of Education set in motion a nationwide antibullying campaign.

A series of shootings in U.S. schools in the 1990s raised the stakes even higher. The 1999 massacre at Columbine High School in Littleton, Colorado, triggered widespread

In the aftermath of the 1999 Columbine High School shooting, many wondered whether the bullying the shooters experienced had played a role.

concern about bullying. Two Columbine students shot and killed 12 peers and one teacher before ending their own lives. A leading theory held that the gunmen had sought revenge against bullies. Over the following year, the federal government investigated 37 acts of school violence between 1974 and 2000. Findings revealed that more than 70 percent of the attackers had been victims of bullying.

European writers Neil Marr and Tim Field published a book in 2001 exposing a disturbing trend of teen suicides following struggles with bullying. In the United States in 2010, the rising number of bullying-related suicides brought increasing urgency to the problem.

Families and educators around the world were seeing a different and darker side of bullying. They saw that in extreme cases bullying could claim lives. They began thinking of bullying as a potentially deadly threat to children's safety.

Who Is at Risk?

Today nearly one-third of middle and high school students experience bullying. A 2011 study by the National Center for Education Statistics found 28 percent of students between the ages of 12 and 18 had been bullied at school.

Cyberbullying

Cyberbullying happens when children use electronic devices, such as phones or computers, to bully others. This relatively new kind of bullying can involve sending mean text messages or e-mails. It includes posting hurtful comments on social networking or other websites. Passing around embarrassing photos or videos is another form of cyberbullying. The rise of cyberbullying means kids are at risk whenever they have access to a phone, computer, or tablet.

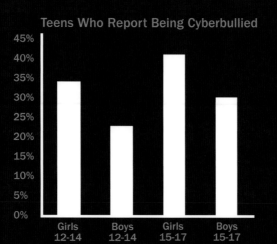

Teens Who Report Being Cyberbullied

Students who are most at risk are seen as different from their peers in some way. The differences can be physical, such as being big or small or having a physical disability. Mental and behavioral differences can also play a role. Many people who bully pick out victims with cultural or lifestyle differences. Children who simply have more trouble making friends or don't do as well in school are also at risk.

Gender identity is a major risk factor for students. Lesbian, gay, bisexual, and transgender (LGBT) youth are much more likely to be bullied than their straight peers. According to the Gay, Lesbian & Straight Education Network's 2011 survey, 82 percent of LGBT youth were verbally harassed in the year before. Nearly two in five reported being physically abused. Straight kids who are perceived as LGBT, such as girls who like stereotypically "boy stuff" and boys who like "girl stuff," may also become victims.

Bullied children are more likely to suffer from anxiety, depression, and other health problems. They often do poorly in school because they worry about staying safe. Bullied students are also more likely to skip classes or drop out of school altogether. Parents of bullied children know better than anyone how serious bullying can be. And they believe the children who bully—not the victims— should pay the price.

Chapter 3

SOMETHING MUST BE DONE

When kids tell adults about bullying, often not much is done. Some parents and teachers ignore bullying and encourage kids to ignore it too. They believe the bullies are looking for a reaction or attention, and if they don't get it, they will stop. Others blame the victim. They feel the bullied child must be doing something to provoke the attacks or not doing enough to stop them.

Deanna wore "short hair and weird clothes" in middle school. She remembers being excluded, teased, and physically attacked by her peers every day.

Adults must be responsive to reports of bullying
in order to prevent future problems.

When she told her parents, they teased her for not being able
to defend herself against a younger, smaller girl. She said:

"It took me two years to work up the courage to tell [my
parents], and then they just blamed me for not standing
up for myself. So one time, in eighth grade, I fought back
and was suspended because it was the word of seven other
girls against me that I started the fight."

Deanna lost trust in her parents and never again asked
them for help with bullying.

Holding Bullies Responsible

Ignoring bullying often makes the situation worse. It is hard
for children to pretend a bully's behavior doesn't affect

them. The bullies might respond by trying harder to get a reaction. Telling kids to ignore bullies makes them feel as if no one will defend them or hold the bullies responsible for their actions.

Blaming the victim sends the message that some children deserve to be bullied based on the choices they make. Adults might say, "Well, you shouldn't have worn that to school," or "You shouldn't tell other kids things like that," or "They would stop hurting you if you would just fight back!" Statements like these make kids feel at fault and imply they are on their own to deal with bullying. Furthermore, children who retaliate against their bullies may get injured or face punishment for fighting at school.

Adults sometimes tell bullying victims to fight back, but this response can get the victim in more trouble.

Many parents and educators believe it is unfair for victims to shoulder the blame for their own abuse. They argue that children who bully should be the ones suffering negative consequences. They want bullies to be punished. Punishment is a traditional way of stopping unwanted behavior by making the risk greater than the reward. A girl who bullies might get temporary pleasure from stealing her classmate's lunch money. But if she is banned from recess for a week as punishment, the overall experience will be unpleasant. She will be less likely to bully her peers again.

Punishment is widely used to guide human behavior through all stages of life, from time-outs for toddlers to prison sentences for adults. So why should school bullies be an exception? Proponents of punishment believe people who bully will not stop until they face harsh consequences.

How Should Bullies Be Punished?

Concern over the suicides and shootings thought to be related in part to bullying in the 1990s to 2000s highlighted the need to take decisive action against students who bully. Schools across the United States and Europe adopted zero-tolerance policies. The policies issue the same punishment—usually suspension, expulsion, or another severe consequence—for all forms of bullying. Schools believe zero-tolerance policies help deter bullying because the risk of harsh punishment is high. Bullying is never ignored, consequences are consistent, and all children who bully are held accountable to the same degree.

Other schools agree that children who bully should be punished but disagree with the zero-tolerance approach. They feel the punishment should fit the crime. In their view, less severe bullying deserves a less severe punishment. Many schools define various levels of bullying—ranging from name-calling to assault with a weapon. They assign various levels of punishment to each type of bullying. In some schools, students help set rules and consequences they feel are fair.

A low-level punishment might be a verbal warning. A more severe punishment might be a detention. The most severe punishments are usually suspension or expulsion. Supporters believe they are protecting other children's safety by removing the bully from school.

Some believe that in severe cases students who bully should be punished as criminals. This is especially common when bullying is thought to have played a role in a victim's injury or death. Treating bullies as criminals, supporters argue, is a powerful deterrent from bullying. Being found guilty of a crime can carry heavy short-term consequences and lifelong repercussions, which most students would rather avoid.

Punishments such as seeing the principal, suspension, and expulsion are common deterrents to bullying.

HARSHER PENALTIES

Countries and communities around the world are demanding stronger action against people who bully. Some believe firm discipline is part of a larger solution to bullying. Others believe punishment alone is enough to discourage bullies and bring them to justice. Many communities have created policies and laws that call for punishment as a solution to bullying.

The U.S. Gets Tough on Bullying

Since the 1990s many U.S. states and schools have favored strict consequences for bullying. After the Columbine shootings in 1999, Georgia was the first state to introduce antibullying laws. Every state but Montana had enacted such laws by 2014. No federal

Communities are getting serious about stopping bullying.

law yet addresses bullying specifically, so each state has its
own laws and policies.

Most states agree that punishment is at least part of the
necessary response to bullying. Many state laws spell out
required punishments, although not all do. Many states
additionally have written model policies for districts
to adopt.

A report by the U.S. Department of Education in
2011 analyzed the policies of 20 large school districts
randomly selected from 19 states across the country. The
analysis found that all 20 districts support consequences
or disciplinary actions for students who bully. Half the
districts "focus largely on punitive actions that often
include suspension, expulsion, transfer to alternative

Antibullying Laws and Policies by State

State Has Antibullying Laws Only
State Government Provides Model Antibullying Policies Only
State Has Antibullying Laws and Policies

programs, or denial of participation in extracurricular or co-curricular activities." The other half rely on a wider range of solutions, including counseling.

Georgia remains one of the toughest states on school bullying. According to its antibullying law, a student who has bullied others three times in one school year must be expelled and moved to a different school. A number of laws in other states—including Alaska, California, Nebraska, and New Jersey—call for suspension, expulsion, and sometimes reporting to law enforcement.

Criminalization of Bullying

The Department of Education also noted that many states are working to make bullying a crime. At least three states have defined specific bullying behaviors as crimes. Others have changed existing laws to apply to bullying behaviors. Some forms of bullying, such as stalking and battery, already break existing laws. Criminal charges are especially common when bullying appears to influence a child to commit suicide.

Twenty-year-old Dharun Ravi was sentenced to 30 days in jail and 300 hours of community service and fined $10,000 in 2012 for bullying-related crimes in New Jersey. He had used a webcam to secretly watch his gay roommate, Tyler Clementi, interact with another man in

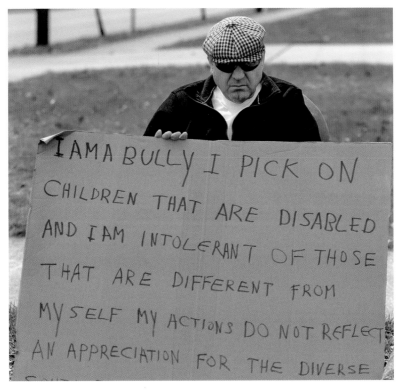

Some communities pass creative sentences to deter bullying. An Ohio man was required by a judge to sit with a sign for hours because he harassed a neighborhood child with disabilities.

2010. Then Ravi posted about the encounter online. Days later Clementi died by suicide. Clementi's death motivated New Jersey to pass some of the nation's toughest laws against bullying.

Several more young people faced criminal charges in 2013 for bullying classmates. Two Florida teens were charged with felony stalking after the target of their cyberbullying, 12-year-old Rebecca, took her own life. The felony charges were later dropped, but the bullies still faced public scrutiny and possible consequences in juvenile court. Rebecca's death has led Florida lawmakers to consider making bullying a crime.

The same year three white California college students collared their black roommate with a bicycle lock. They performed other vicious acts of race-related bullying as well. They were charged with hate crimes and battery and may face jail time. Fortunately, their roommate survived the attacks. His family wants the bullies to be convicted.

Fighting Bullies Around the World

After the flurry of antibullying legislation in the United States, several Canadian provinces followed suit. Alberta lawmakers passed a bill in 2012 that would allow for suspension or expulsion not only of bullies but also of bystanders who chose not to report or act on the bullying. In some Alberta cities, people who bully can be fined up to

$1,000 or put in jail. Proponents of the laws feel the strict measures will quickly reduce bullying.

In the United Kingdom, bullying behaviors including repeated name-calling, cyberbullying, physical violence, and hate crimes are illegal. The country encourages victims and bystanders to report the behaviors to the police. In addition, the law requires all UK public schools to have policies against bullying.

Bullying has also become a severe problem in South Korean schools, where a competitive and high-stakes school environment may fuel the behavior. Suicide is the leading cause of death for South Korean teens and preteens, and bullying is believed to be a major factor in the deaths. The government responded in 2012 with harsher penalties, including suspensions and a note in

Cyberbullying Laws

Cyberbullying has become a serious concern for many schools and families. Educators have the authority to deal with bullying that happens on school grounds. But cyberbullying often happens outside of school. So who should be responsible for stopping it?

Several U.S. states have passed or proposed laws to protect victims of cyberbullying. Some laws give schools power to intervene in cyberbullying only when it happens at school or during school-related activities. Other laws say that when cyberbullying interferes with education, schools should take action even if the cyberbullying itself happens outside of school. In states without cyberbullying laws, some schools still take action no matter when or where cyberbullying happens. Others feel they have no right to intervene outside of school, and that responsibility should fall to parents or police.

bullies' permanent records. The government further announced that any child age 12 or older could face criminal charges for bullying.

Is Punishment the Solution?

Today most communities agree bullying is a serious form of abuse that cannot be tolerated. And in many homes and schools, punishment is viewed as the traditional and reliable approach to stopping bullying and other unwanted behaviors. Since the 1990s global antibullying policies and laws have shown that numerous schools, states, provinces, and countries believe in the effectiveness of punishment.

Most antibullying programs and laws have been implemented recently and include varied definitions of and responses to bullying. That makes it difficult for researchers to determine which methods are most effective.

However, a 2011 study found that firm disciplinary methods appeared to be one of the most important elements in an effective program. Even programs not based on punishment, such as Norway's Olweus Bullying Prevention Program, recognize that some negative consequences are necessary to stop bullying. The findings lend support to proponents of punishment and their powerful stance against bullying.

WHAT DO YOU THINK?

- Should all people who bully receive the same severe punishment, or should each punishment fit the crime? Why do you think so?

- What do you think is an appropriate punishment for physical bullying? Verbal bullying? Cyberbullying? Other types of bullying?

- If you were the bully, how do you think you would respond to each type of punishment?

- Would your opinions about punishing bullies change if you were a bullying victim? How so, and why?

- Do you think schools have a right to punish students for cyberbullying that happens outside of school? Why or why not?

INDEX

GLOSSARY

antisocial personality disorder—a condition involving a lack of consideration for others' feelings, rights, and safety

anxiety—a feeling of fear, worry, or nervousness about something that might happen

battery—the crime of unwanted physical contact or use of force against someone

bully-victim—a child who is sometimes bullied and sometimes bullies others

depression—a condition that causes long-term feelings of sadness, hopelessness, and worthlessness

empathy—the ability to understand and share others' feelings

felony—a serious crime, such as murder

proponent—a person who argues in favor of something

retaliate—to get revenge against someone who you feel has harmed you

INTERNET SITES

Use FactHound to find Internet sites related to this book. All of the sites on FactHound have been researched by our staff.

Here's all you do:
Visit *www.facthound.com*
Type in this code: 9780756549954

PROS AND CONS: ZERO TOLERANCE

Pros

Quick way of dealing with bullying

Satisfying to see bullies receive negative consequences

Thought to deter bullying

Holds bullies responsible for their actions

Traditional way of correcting unwanted behavior

Cons

Can make bullies feel resentful and more likely to misbehave

Suspension or expulsion can make bullies feel isolated and unsupported

Suspension and expulsion increase the risk of future criminal behavior and decrease academic success

Does not teach alternative, more positive behaviors

Severe punishments make teachers and students less likely to report bullying

PROS AND CONS: WORKING TOGETHER

Pros

Supports all students involved in conflict, including bullies and bystanders

Thought to prevent bullying by creating a positive, respectful school environment

Holds bullies responsible for their actions

Builds social, emotional, and problem-solving skills

Promotes relationships of respect and trust between teachers and students, making students more likely to ask for help

Effectiveness is supported by research

Cons

May not be effective in all situations

Takes significant amounts of time, effort, and money to implement

Takes time away from teaching academic subjects

Some may feel this approach is too easy on bullies

CRITICAL THINKING USING THE COMMON CORE

1. Consider both perspectives presented in this book. Each side uses examples that support its argument. Identify an example used by both perspectives. How does each side use the example to support its arguments? Which side uses the example more effectively? (Craft and Structure)

2. What approach to bullying does your school take? Using arguments and examples from this book, build a plan for how you think your school's antibullying efforts could be improved. (Key Ideas and Details)

3. After reading both perspectives, what component of an antibullying program do you think is the most effective? Why? (Integration of Knowledge and Ideas)

BOOKS IN THIS SERIES

Animal Testing: Lifesaving Research vs. Animal Welfare

Punishing Bullies: Zero Tolerance vs. Working Together

School Lunches: Healthy Choices vs. Crowd Pleasers

Social Media: Like It or Leave It

III

FURTHER READING

Asher, Jay. *Th1rteen R3asons Why: A Novel.* New York: Razorbill, 2007.

Hall, Megan Kelley, and Carrie Jones, eds. *Dear Bully: 70 Authors Tell Their Stories.* New York: HarperTeen, 2011.

Lohmann, Raychelle Cassada. *The Bullying Workbook for Teens: Activities to Help You Deal with Social Aggression and Cyberbullying.* Oakland, Calif.: New Harbinger Publications, 2013.

Meyers, Stephanie H., et al., eds. *Bullying Under Attack: True Stories Written by Teen Victims, Bullies, and Bystanders.* Deerfield Beach, Fla.: Health Communications, 2013.

SELECT BIBLIOGRAPHY

"Are Zero Tolerance Policies Effective in the Schools?" American Psychological Association. December 2008. 1 July 2014. http://www.apa.org/pubs/info/reports/zero-tolerance.pdf

Bazelon, Emily. *Sticks and Stones: Defeating the Culture of Bullying and Rediscovering the Power of Character and Empathy.* New York: Random House, 2013.

Bully. Dir. Lee Hirsch. The Weinstein Company and Where We Live Films, 2011.

Goldman, Carrie. *Bullied: What Every Parent, Teacher, and Kid Needs to Know about Ending the Cycle of Fear.* New York: HarperOne, 2012.

Hirsch, Lee, Cynthia Lowen, and Dina Santorelli, eds. *Bully: An Action Plan for Teachers and Parents to Combat the Bullying Crisis.* New York: Weinstein Books, 2012.

Miller, Cindy, and Cynthia Lowen. *The Essential Guide to Bullying Prevention and Intervention: Protecting Children and Teens from Physical, Emotional, and Online Bullying.* New York: Alpha Books, 2012.

Sacco, Dina T., et al. "An Overview of State Antibullying Legislation and Other Related Laws." The Berkman Center for Internet and Society at Harvard University. 23 Feb. 2012. 1 July 2014. http://cyber.law.harvard.edu/sites/cyber.law.harvard.edu/files/State_Anti_bullying_Legislation_Overview_0.pdf

A Perspectives Flip Book

PUNISHING BULLIES:

Zero Tolerance vs.

Working Together

by Lisa Owings

Content Consultant
Amanda B. Nickerson, PhD
Associate Professor and Director
Alberti Center for Bullying Abuse Prevention
University at Buffalo, State University of New York

COMPASS POINT BOOKS
a capstone imprint

ABOUT THE AUTHOR

Lisa Owings has a degree in English and creative writing from the University of Minnesota. She has written and edited a wide variety of educational books for young people. Lisa lives in Andover, Minnesota, with her husband and a small menagerie of pets.

SOURCE NOTES

Zero Tolerance

Page 5, line 23: Lee Hirsch, Cynthia Lowen, and Dina Santorelli, eds. *Bully: An Action Plan for Teachers and Parents to Combat the Bullying Crisis.* New York: Weinstein Books, 2012, p. 28.

Page 6, line 9: Emily Bazelon. *Sticks and Stones: Defeating the Culture of Bullying and Rediscovering the Power of Character and Empathy.* New York: Random House, 2013, p. 61.

Page 8, line 8: Ibid., p. 99.

Page 16, line 9: Carrie Goldman. *Bullied: What Every Parent, Teacher, and Kid Needs to Know about Ending the Cycle of Fear.* New York: HarperOne, 2012, p. 125.

Page 17, line 3: Ibid.

Page 19, sidebar, line 7: *Bully: An Action Plan for Teachers and Parents to Combat the Bullying Crisis,* p. 72.

Page 23, line 13: "Analysis of State Bullying Laws and Policies." U.S. Department of Education. December 2011. 1 July 2014. https://www2. ed.gov/rschstat/eval/bullying/state-bullying-laws/state-bullying-laws.pdf

Working Together

Page 6, line 7: *Bullied: What Every Parent, Teacher, and Kid Needs to Know about Ending the Cycle of Fear,* p. 216.

Page 8, sidebar, line 8: *Sticks and Stones: Defeating the Culture of Bullying and Rediscovering the Power of Character and Empathy,* p. 176.

Page 21, line 23: *Bullied: What Every Parent, Teacher, and Kid Needs to Know about Ending the Cycle of Fear,* p. 234.

Page 26, sidebar, line 18: Ibid., p. 220.

TABLE OF CONTENTS

BEING THE BULLY

A SYMPTOM OF A LARGER PROBLEM

A HOLISTIC APPROACH

WHAT DO YOU THINK?

I
Glossary
& Internet Sites

II
Pros and Cons

III
Critical Thinking Using
the Common Core

IV
Select Bibliography &
Further Reading

BEING THE BULLY

I n almost every school across the globe, some kids bully others. At a basic level, bullying is related to an individual's drive to survive, as well as society's desire to enforce norms and hierarchies. Children see bullies in their lives and bullies in the media, and many mirror their behavior. Children from every culture experience the behavior.

Despite the fact that bullying is a learned behavior, bullies are often thought of as bad kids. Their parents might get easily frustrated with them. Teachers expect them to misbehave and might be more likely to punish them, treat them with disrespect, or give up on trying to help them. Other adults in the community might call for them to be punished, exclude them from group activities, or forbid them to play with their children.

People who bully might not realize how hurtful their actions can be.

Some children who bully are also picked on by their peers, continuing the cycle of bullying.

In addition to facing harshness and isolation from their communities, children who bully often struggle with problems at home, low self-esteem, or disorders that make it difficult for them to control their behavior and emotions. Worst of all, children who bully face a higher risk of becoming criminals and abusers in adulthood.

Bullies' Stories

Some kids bully to make themselves feel better. One boy was overweight, and teasing and pushing smaller kids made him feel powerful and confident. The popular kids

Many people who bully feel lonely or excluded themselves or face other personal or family problems.

at school were accepting of him, and he felt they even encouraged his behavior. He also loved the adrenalin rush bullying gave him. Over the years, the boy became more aggressive. He even brought a knife to school once. His school tried to get him help, but it didn't work. The boy continued his aggressive behavior through high school. "Every time I was caught bullying," he recalled as an adult, "the interventions were punitive, and that didn't work. No one ever tried a positive intervention with me."

When the bullying wasn't enough to make him feel better, he turned to drugs. It was not until years later that he finally sought therapy to help him find happiness and cope with challenges in healthier ways.

Another boy was in therapy from a very young age, but he still had trouble controlling his aggression toward others. By the age of 3, it was clear he needed help solving his behavioral problems. He had to switch to a different preschool that could handle his aggression. On the second day of kindergarten, he pushed another boy off the playground equipment. The boy fell on his face and got a horrible bruise. The young bully continued to be aggressive toward the boy both inside and outside of school. Over time, with the support of his school and the guidance of a social worker, the young bully's behavior and relationships improved.

Relationship conflicts led a group of high school girls in Massachusetts to bully. A new girl in school had formed relationships with two of the girls' boyfriends, and the girls didn't like it. They responded by calling the new girl filthy names and spreading rumors about her on Facebook. Then they began bullying her at school and threatening to beat her up. They were shocked when they learned she had died by suicide.

The media and the public held the bullies responsible for the new girl's death. The girls were charged with

multiple felony crimes and faced up to 10 years in prison. Putting together the stories afterward, it remains unclear to what extent the girls' interaction was bullying rather than the relationship-related drama that is fairly common in high schools. Experts and the public debate whether the harsh charges were appropriate. The most serious charges were eventually dropped, but the girls faced community service, probation, public humiliation, harassment, and an extended absence from school.

Bullying is never the right thing to do. But that doesn't mean it's always black and white. Bullying is a complex behavior. Many would argue it requires a complex

Bullied to Death?

The media can be quick to blame bullies when victimized youths commit suicide. Research shows bullying does not cause suicide. Rather, it is usually one of several risk factors. In the new girl's case, records of her long history with depression and a previous suicide attempt suggested other factors were at play. The girl had also been struggling with her parents' separation and conflict with her mother. "If you bully someone to death, that's murder," explained criminal law professor Joseph Kennedy. "But if you bully someone, and then they kill themselves, and that's not something you anticipated, that's not a crime."

solution—more complex than doling out harsh, uniform punishments that don't necessarily fit the crime.

The kids in these stories—kids who bully—are not bad kids. They are imperfect, and they are still learning and developing. They don't always know the right way to express their feelings. The new girl's bullies struggled with feelings of betrayal, jealousy, and anger. They expressed these feelings in ways that hurt others. But did they deserve to be treated as murderers?

Many believe people who bully should be punished severely and to the full extent of the law. However, others argue that harsh punishments don't do bullies any good. They don't teach children how to cope with emotions and conflicts in healthy ways. These people believe a positive solution would be more effective.

Many argue bullies need help learning better ways to cope with their emotions.

A SYMPTOM OF A LARGER PROBLEM

Countries, states, and schools have their own definitions of bullying. Most agree that behavior has to be intentional for it to be considered bullying. If a child is joking around and accidentally hurts someone's feelings, then he or she is not a bully. Bullying is also not usually a onetime event. The behaviors are repeated over time. In addition, people who bully have physical or emotional power over their victims. Sometimes bullies don't recognize the power imbalance. They believe the person they are harming is able to fight back on equal footing. In reality their victim is powerless to stand up for himself or herself.

Peer pressure can make kids feel they must choose between being bullied or becoming a bully.

Bullying takes many forms. It can be physical, such as hitting or tripping someone. It can also be verbal, such as calling someone names or threatening to hurt them. Sometimes physical and verbal bullying start as pranks or good-natured teasing. It is easy to get carried away and take things too far. Or if others are physically or verbally bullying someone, it may seem easier and safer to go along with the group than to take a stand with the victim.

Social bullying happens when kids try to harm others' friendships. They might spread hurtful rumors, exclude

someone from the group, or publicly humiliate someone. Kids often feel pressured into social bullying. If a child's friends are bullying someone, she might think she will lose their friendship if she does not participate.

Cyberbullying can take place almost anytime, anywhere. Rumors, insults, photos, and videos can spread much faster online than in person. Bullies can keep their identities hidden. And it can be hard or impossible to delete hurtful messages or images. People who bully online may not realize how much they are hurting their victims because they are not face-to-face. And it's easy to

Many children need extra support to break out of a pattern of bullying behavior.

participate in cyberbullying just by clicking *send.* These things make cyberbullying one of the most serious forms of bullying.

Both Sides of the Equation

Bullying is a serious problem with severe consequences for victims. Victims of bullying need help and protection. But people who seek a positive solution for bullying argue that bullies need help too. Children who bully others are more likely to be experiencing problems at home, such as neglectful, abusive, or distant parents. Some children who bully have low self-esteem and use bullying to make themselves look more powerful. Bullies can also be bullied themselves. Kids who switch roles between bully and victim are called bully-victims.

Some children have natural tendencies to be more aggressive. Others have disabilities that make it more difficult for them to control their emotions and aggressive impulses. These children are more likely to bully others. The struggles they face are made worse when friends, parents, and teachers ignore or accidentally encourage bullying behavior.

Bully-victims face a higher risk of developing mental health problems such as depression, anxiety disorders, and antisocial personality disorder. People who bully are also more likely to abuse drugs and alcohol, drop out of

school, and become criminals. One study showed that 40 percent of boys who bullied others in middle school had committed three or more crimes by the time they turned 24. In addition, people who bully are more likely to abuse their partners, children, and other loved ones when they grow up.

Bully Culture

Children are not born bullies. They learn how to bully, and they continue the behavior as long as it gets them what they want. In today's society bullying behaviors are frequently modeled and encouraged. Children may learn bullying from their parents, siblings, or friends—or even their teachers.

Kelby's Story

Lesbian teen Kelby struggled through years of teasing and violent attacks that drove her to attempt suicide three times. Her peers, their families, her basketball teammates, and even her teachers—most of whom were devoutly Christian—believed being gay was a sin. All but her family and a few close friends silently tolerated or approved of her being bullied. One of the hardest things for Kelby was that some of her teachers, who were supposed to support and protect her, participated in her bullying by making rude remarks about her sexual orientation in front of the entire class. The teachers' comments made Kelby's bullies feel they were doing the right thing. Though Kelby's parents were willing to move to a more accepting place, Kelby—now transgender—decided to stay in his own community and drive change at both the local and national levels.

Nearly all forms of media teach bullying. Movies and television often send the message that violence earns admiration. Comedies, reality TV shows, and other types of shows make verbal and social bullying seem entertaining and acceptable. One study has shown that kids who watch a lot of reality TV are more likely to believe that bullying is OK and that it can help them get ahead in life. Research also suggests that violent video games make children more likely to engage in violent behavior, including bullying, in real life. Even music is often filled with language that encourages discrimination, violence, and sexual harassment.

Many children are taught through their culture or religion that certain races, religions, sexual orientations, or ways of life are "other" or wrong. Such attitudes make it harder for these kids to relate to those who break social, cultural, or gender norms and thus make bullying more likely. Parents and teachers often unintentionally reward children for bullying those who go outside these perceived boundaries.

Growing numbers of parents and educators believe more needs to be done to counteract this culture of bullying. They argue that punishing responds to bullying with more bullying. They believe schools should instead work to teach children empathy, tolerance, and healthy ways to express their feelings.

A HOLISTIC APPROACH

Bullying arises from a variety of factors. But that does not mean bullying is ever acceptable. People who want to find a positive solution to bullying still believe it needs to stop. They simply believe punishment is not the most effective way to achieve that goal.

Punishing children who bully may seem like a straightforward and satisfying approach. But some research has shown that harsh punishments make the problem worse. Punishment on its own tells children they are doing something wrong, but it does not teach them alternative behaviors.

Many schools are beginning antibullying programs that focus on fostering respect over punishing bad behavior.

Both children and adults are less likely to report bullying if the child who bullied would automatically be suspended or expelled. Children often fear the bully's retaliation, and adults may think the punishment does not fit the behavior. Especially if the punishment is severe, bullies tend to feel they are being treated unfairly and may act out more as a result. In addition, if the bully thinks his victim has tattled on him, he is likely to seek revenge.

Increasing numbers of schools across the globe are implementing policies that focus less on punishing students who bully. Instead, they prevent bullying by teaching students to treat others with kindness.

These schools create a positive environment that encourages respect and appreciation for differences.

Preventing Bullying

The first step in many prevention programs involves teaching both adults and students what bullying is. They learn how to recognize it and how to respond to it—including when it happens online. They learn that bullying is unacceptable. Children learn to ask adults for help. They also learn how to reduce their chances of being targeted. They practice supporting peers who are bullied.

Adults learn to demonstrate and reward positive behaviors. They set fair consequences that help children reflect on their behavior and how it affects others. They provide more supervision, as well as healthy outlets for frustration, such as physical activity. Good relationships with teachers make students want to follow the rules. Students who sense their teachers are on their side are also more likely to ask for help.

In addition, prevention programs often teach positive social and emotional skills. Teaching kids to appreciate one another's differences is important for preventing bullying. If children know how to relate to people who are different, schools will become safer places.

One way children can learn to understand other people's emotions is through empathy-building exercises.

Group songs in schools build trust and empathy between students.

For example, say a child is bullied because she is blind. The teacher might have the rest of the class put on blindfolds while they attempt everyday activities. This exercise would help them understand the challenges students who are blind face and how they feel.

Social skills such as communicating effectively and resolving conflicts can help kids stop bullying before it starts. For example, saying "I felt sad when you didn't let me sit with you" is more likely to help resolve conflict than saying "You're so mean!" Students can also learn how body language can help them avoid or resolve conflict.

Counseling

Sometimes children involved in bullying need extra help. They might be experiencing problems at home. Or they might have mental or physical disabilities that make them more likely to bully or be a target of bullying. Such students may benefit from talking to a school counselor, social worker, psychologist, or psychiatrist. These kinds of therapy help students get to the root of their social issues and find healthy solutions.

Positive Interventions

No matter how much effort schools put into bullying prevention, bullying will happen sometimes. Many schools have come up with positive ways to intervene when it does.

Adults can help victims of bullying by building their self-confidence, teaching them to be assertive, and showing them ways to stay calm and positive in the face of bullying. For example, standing up straight, looking the bully in the eye, and telling her firmly but calmly to stop can work. Victims can try explaining to bullies how the behavior makes them feel. They are also encouraged to tell an adult.

Adults can help children who bully accept responsibility for their actions. They can reward honesty. They can also let the child know there will be further investigation into what happened. If the bully learns to be honest with himself and others about his behavior, he will likely be less resentful of consequences and more willing to acknowledge that his bullying hurt others. Consequences such as making a sincere apology or replacing a broken item can help right the wrong. Consequences such as community service or volunteer work are helpful in teaching responsibility, humility, and empathy.

Teachers and parents can also teach children who bully how to manage their emotions in healthy ways. They can explain that it is OK to feel anger and frustration, but it is never OK to bully. Then they can offer alternative activities for kids to vent their negative emotions, such as taking an art class to express themselves or joining a sports team.

Restorative Justice

Some schools have found that a strategy called restorative justice works to repair relationships between children who bully and their victims. The strategy builds a personal connection between children. Brenda Morrison, director of Canada's Centre for Restorative Justice, says this strategy "is not about punishment and rules; it is about values and relationships." Restorative justice takes a different form for

each bullying relationship. It usually involves the bully, the victim, and a group of supporters for each. Each person shares his or her feelings about what happened. Everyone listens respectfully to all others in the group. Often the bully and victim also share personal information that helps them get to know each other and builds empathy between them.

The group comes up with a plan to stop the bullying and heal the relationship in a positive way. In one instance, the victim's parent was a dance teacher, and the bully loved to dance. The boys decided to resolve their conflict by taking a dance class together. Finding an activity they could both enjoy set them on the path to friendship.

Restorative justice takes time and must be done well. Putting the bully and the victim together can be risky, and the situation must be handled carefully. More studies are needed to judge the effectiveness of the program in a wider range of locations.

Helping Bystanders

Not every child bullies or is bullied. But most children know what bullying looks like and have seen it firsthand. Witnesses to bullying are called bystanders. Even if they don't support bullying, the vast majority of bystanders don't know how to stop it. Schools that support a positive

approach to bullying often teach bystanders to become more active in stopping bullying or supporting victims.

Bystanders are encouraged to report bullying behavior to adults. Those who are confident enough to stand up to bullies are encouraged to do so. They can tell the bully to stop, verbally defend the victim, or help the victim get away. If bystanders believe standing up to the bully would not be safe, they can support the victim afterward by befriending him and letting him know they do not agree with what happened. Bystanders can also refuse to participate in spreading rumors. They can stop forwarding inappropriate pictures or videos or laughing when people get bullied. Involving bystanders—including adults—makes bullying prevention a schoolwide effort.

A key to ending the culture of bullying is teaching bystanders positive ways to react—rather than watching passively or contributing to the problem.

FRIENDLIER SCHOOLS

After a rash of school shootings and bullying-related suicides in the late 1990s, American schools worked urgently to crack down on bullying. Many turned to strict zero-tolerance policies, issuing harsh punishments for all bullying incidents. Since 1999 more and more countries, states, and towns have passed laws that require tough consequences for people who bully.

Research has since shown that the strong policies often do not reduce bullying. In fact, harsh punishments such as suspensions and expulsions seemed to increase misbehavior and decrease success in school. As a result many schools and communities

Bullying-related deaths have led some communities to crack down harshly on bullying, but some experts do not believe that is the answer.

around the world have sought more positive solutions to bullying.

The Olweus Bullying Prevention Program

Swedish-born psychology professor Dan Olweus was the first to develop a schoolwide positive approach to bullying prevention. His program was based on bullying research he did in the 1970s. It was created in response to the tragic bullying-related suicides of three young Norwegian boys in 1982. Large-scale evaluations showed the Olweus Bullying Prevention Program (OBPP) decreased bullying in Norwegian schools by approximately 50 percent.

The program is widely used in schools throughout Europe and the United States, although it has not proven as effective as in Norway. The OBPP strives to create a positive school environment in which students and adults care about and respect one another. Educators are more concerned with rewarding positive behavior and helping students repair relationships than with doling out punishments. Children who bully, victims, and bystanders all receive support.

Inspiring Positive Solutions

More than 8,000 schools in the United States alone have adopted Olweus' program. Experts have also developed other positive programs, each with its own unique approach. These include Second Step, KiVa, and Positive Behavioral Interventions and Supports (PBIS). Schools around the world have adapted the programs to their own

True Story: Finding Empathy

Ross was a high school bully. He was particularly mean to one student until his teachers and peers banded together to discourage the bullying. A couple of years later, Ross learned the student he had bullied had attempted suicide. He finally understood how this boy must have felt, and the guilt was overwhelming. Ross tried to make amends for what he had done. He started saying hi to his former victim in the halls, and the boy responded with smiles. In a book that collected stories about bullying, Ross confessed, "That was thirty years ago ... But I like to think that I have never forgotten the lesson that he didn't ever realize he had taught me."

Students in the Olweus program sign an antibullying pledge.

needs. Some programs are highly structured. Others are
more flexible. The common thread is giving both students
and educators the social, emotional, and problem-solving
tools they need to prevent and respond to bullying.

Change in the United States

The U.S. Department of Education published guidelines
for educators in January 2014 that strongly recommended
taking a positive approach to bullying. The U.S.
Department of Health and Human Services also created an
antibullying website that promotes positive approaches
and consequences to address bullying. California, Florida,
Massachusetts, New Jersey, and other states recommend
counseling bullies and victims to help address the
behavior on a deeper level. Ten states require schools to

use positive interventions. A bill called the Safe Schools Improvement Act has been introduced in Congress. It details Congress' finding that using positive interventions for bullying keeps kids in school and out of the juvenile justice system.

Are Positive Strategies the Solution?

Positive antibullying policies have become popular, but researchers are still debating their effectiveness. Studies are difficult to conduct and have shown mixed results. However, evidence suggests that several positive programs, such as the OBPP and KiVa, can be effective under the right conditions. Supporters feel the research on positive programs is promising enough to adopt this approach to bullying. Research aside, many communities simply feel better about focusing on positive behaviors and supportive interventions than on negative behaviors and punishments. Given the known problems with zero-tolerance and other punitive policies, they believe more positive approaches are at least a step in the right direction.

WHAT DO YOU THINK?

- Complete this sentence: People who bully should _____ [never/always/sometimes] be punished for their actions. Why?

- If you were a school principal, how would you stop bullying in your school?

- A popular boy at your school shoves another boy into some lockers in the hallway. The boy he pushes is carrying a pink lunch bag.

  - How do you think the popular boy feels? What would be the best way to stop him from bullying?

  - How do you think the victim feels? What should he do in this situation?

  - How do you think bystanders could help?

INDEX